THE GIRLS' YOGA BOOK

Stretch Your Body, Open Your Mind, & Have Fun!

Written by Michaela Caldwell
Illustrations by Claudia Dávila

MAPLE
TREE
PRESS

Maple Tree Press Inc.
51 Front Street East, Suite 200, Toronto, Ontario M5E 1B3
www.mapletreepress.com

Distributed in Canada by Raincoast Books
9050 Shaughnessy Street, Vancouver, British Columbia V6P 6E5

Distributed in the United States by Publishers Group West
1700 Fourth Street, Berkeley, California 94710

Dedication

*To my family and friends—for believing in me and inspiring me every day.
And to all teachers who encourage others to explore their bodies and minds through
the gift of yoga, especially Esther Myers, whose inspiration lives on.*

Cataloguing in Publication Data
Caldwell, Michaela
     The girls' yoga book : stretch your body, open your mind & have fun! / Michaela Caldwell ;
Claudia Dávila, illustrator.

(Girl zone)
Includes index.
ISBN 1-897066-24-4 (bound).   ISBN 1-897066-25-2 (pbk.)

     1. Yoga—Juvenile literature. 2. Girls—Health and hygiene—Juvenile literature.
I. Dávila, Claudia II. Title. III. Series.

RA781.7.C24 2005   j613.7'046'08342   C2004-905588-7

Design & Art Direction: Claudia Dávila
Illustrations: Claudia Dávila

We acknowledge the financial support of the Canada Council for the Arts, the Ontario
Arts Council, the Government of Canada through the Book Publishing Industry
Development Program (BPIDP), and the Government of Ontario through the Ontario
Media Development Corporation's Book Initiative for our publishing activities.

ONTARIO ARTS COUNCIL
CONSEIL DES ARTS DE L'ONTARIO

Printed in Belgium

B   C   D   E   F

CONTENTS

AMAZING YOGINI

Girls are so amazing! Sometimes it must feel like you are carrying a heavy weight on your shoulders with so many pressures in your life—school, friends, family, and everything else going on in the world around you. But still, you manage to grow and sparkle through it all. Maybe you could use a little help shrugging off some stress, so that you can feel confident and glow with good health. This book will show you new ways to relax and let go of some of those pressures you feel—and have tons of fun while you're at it.

Yoga helps you discover the whole you. It can help you understand and explore the different parts of yourself: your body (the physical parts of you), your mind (how you feel and what you think), and your spirit (your personality, the spark that makes you unique). Yoga is about joining these three parts together to make a unique, special, and beautiful person inside and out.

A girl who practices yoga is called a yogini. Yogini sounds like genie. Magical things can happen when you do yoga. You can feel and see changes in your body, your mind, your personality, and your outlook on the world. Be a yogini and experience the magic!

Girl Talk

We asked some girls to share their thoughts on yoga, how it helps their lives, and fun things they do to relax. Check out the Girl Talks throughout this book to find great tips for how you can fit yoga into your daily life.

WHAT IS YOGA?

Yoga was developed in India over 5,000 years ago. Since then, yoga has traveled all over the world, becoming very popular recently in many places outside of India. The word "yoga" means "union"—it links your body, your breath, and your mind.

Yoga was first practiced by men (yogis) who went into the woods to meditate for years. Sitting all day was hard work, so they realized that they felt better if they also stretched. They developed poses that helped them with their aches and pains, and to think more clearly... and yoga was born! Although most of us aren't sitting and meditating all day, we can all use some help stretching and thinking.

Though its ancient roots are spiritual, yoga is not a religion. It has been many things to many people, including a spiritual source, exercise for the body, and a way to quiet their thoughts. You can decide what it is for you.

Sanskrit is an ancient language of India. A lot of yoga terms come from Sanskrit. In this book, we have used the Western words to describe the yoga poses, but sometimes you'll see some traditional words, too. You might find it fun to experiment with the lovely sounds of this language by saying the Sanskrit words aloud.

Asana (pronounced AH-sah-nah) is the Sanskrit word for the physical postures of yoga. The poses, or asanas, in this book are beginner poses, and should be practiced with safety in mind. Take care to follow the instructions, and talk to a yoga teacher or other adult before trying a pose that you are unsure of. Always pay special attention to your neck, knees, lower back, and wrists.

Say Ohm!

A lot of people think of the sound "ohm" when they think of yoga. If you say it aloud, it can feel great vibrating through your body. Try it out for yourself. Take a deep breath in. As you breathe out, open your mouth wide and exhale the sound "Aaaahh…." Still breathing out, make an "O" with your mouth and exhale the sound "Oooohh…." Closing your lips, finish the breath by exhaling the sound "Mmmmmm…." This is often done by everyone together at the beginning and end of a yoga class.

Yoga M"ohm"ent

Yoga moments can come before a play, during a test, even while waiting for the bus. It's those times when you need to feel less confused or worried, and more in control of your thoughts and feelings. Taking a yoga moment can be simply taking a deep breath or doing another yoga technique from this book.

Girl Talk

Yoga is...really relaxing. It calms your mind, refreshes you, and makes you feel strong and good about yourself. – Mizzú

YOUR YOGA SPACE

You can do yoga anywhere, anytime. One of the best ways to do yoga is outside, stretching up to the clouds and feeling the delicious sensation of the ground beneath your feet. No equipment is necessary when you have a soft blanket of grass beneath you. Indoors, you don't *have* to have any special equipment either, but there are some things that will help you to create a calm, peaceful oasis.

Yoga M"ohm"ent

Sometimes, while crossing the hot, dry desert, travelers come upon an "oasis," a precious source of water and shade. Stopping and resting at an oasis gives them a chance to unwind, and eat and drink, so that they can continue their travels. An oasis can be anywhere that is peaceful and calm, where you can rest your body and mind.

Set up your yoga space in a spot that is free from noise and distractions.

How to create your yoga scene:

• Turn off any distractions (computer, TV, radio, telephone).

• Try to choose a time when you won't be interrupted.

• Put on some relaxing music, or just enjoy the silence.

• Turn off any bright lights.

• Set up your yoga mat, blanket, and cushion (see opposite page).

• Sit quietly and enjoy the soothing, peaceful space you have made for yourself.

Create Your Yoga Oasis

⭐ What You'll Need ⭐

Sticky Mat

Popular yoga products, mats are available at yoga studios, fitness stores, and even some book and video stores. If you don't have one, make sure you take off your socks, as bare feet help stop you from slipping. Sticky mats are safest, though.

Belt

Belts can help you stretch further in some poses. They're available from yoga and fitness stores, or karate supply stores. You can also just use a belt from a bathrobe.

Blanket

It can be nice to have the comfort of your favorite blanket during the quiet times of yoga. Sometimes as your body relaxes, you can feel a little chilled. A blanket helps you feel cozy, secure, rested, and relaxed.

Bolster (or big cushion)

Cushions give support for your back in seated and lying-down poses.

Girl Talk

My favorite place to relax is my nice, warm, and comfy bed. – Seacy

My favorite place is my room with no sound, where I can release all of my tension, let go of reality, and live in my own world. – Tereka

YOUR BODY

People come in all shapes and sizes— that's what makes us so wonderful and unique. You may be going through a time when your body is growing and changing a great deal. Sometimes it's hard not to compare yourself to others.

Yoga teaches us to listen and respond to our bodies as we breathe and work through different poses. In yoga class or when practicing with someone else, you might be tempted to be competitive. But it's not important that your friend can touch her toes when you can't, or that your heels don't reach the ground in Downward Dog pose (page 35). Yoga isn't just about doing the poses, it's also about learning about your body. By being patient and kind to yourself, you'll be amazed at what your body will be able to do.

Yoga M"ohm"ent

Many cultures believe that there is remarkable power in the hands. Yoga can even be practiced with your hands only, by using hand positions called mudras (pronounced MOO-dras). Mudra means "seal," which refers to the point of contact at the fingertips. In yoga, placing your fingers, thumbs, and palms together in particular ways can change your mood, energy level, and how you are feeling.

Mudra for Energy

Try this mudra (above) to energize you. Touch the pads of your thumb and index finger together lightly to form a circle of energy that stays within your body. Slightly extend your other fingers.

Girl Talk

A girl who feels good about herself looks and acts confident and beautiful no matter what her size, age, or race.

— Kimberly

Beauty doesn't necessarily mean being pretty. It also means being kind. We are all beautiful inside and outside. It's something we should cherish. – Joanna

Energize Your Body

In the yoga tradition, chakras (pronounced SHA-kras) are areas of energy that match up with parts of the body—and certain colors and feelings (see page 21). By concentrating on a particular chakra, or area of the body, you can stimulate the energy and change the feelings associated with that chakra. Try it for yourself with this exercise below.

The heart chakra represents love and compassion. Stand tall and place the palms of your hands together in front of your heart, fingers pointing up. Think about someone you love. Keeping your hands together and fingers pointed up, slowly raise your hands up above your head. Do you have a feeling of energy flowing through your arms? Breathe and let your feelings go.

Yoga M"ohm"ent

Need a pick-me-up or a kick-start to your day? Try a few rounds of Sun Salutations (page 59) in the morning or any time to revive your body, refresh your mind, and brighten your mood.

STAND TALL

A girl who stands tall and straight exudes confidence, strength, and style. Thinking about your body and how to position it is very helpful when you're doing yoga. In yoga we use our own body weight, breath, and concentration to do the poses. So, basically, yoga is your own body helping you get stronger. By being aware of your body, you can learn to do the poses better, since every pose is designed to help out specific parts of you.

Standing straight is good "alignment"—when all the supporting body parts like your spine, limbs, and muscles are all stacked up properly. Alignment in yoga not only helps you do the poses properly, it's also a great beauty tip because you are working on your posture. So go ahead, balance your head, roll back your shoulders, lengthen your spine, and align yourself with confidence.

A girl who feels good about herself is confident, proud of who she is, and doesn't change for anyone but herself. – Megan

Yoga M"ohm"ent

The Ancient Egyptians also thought about good posture and standing tall. Statues of the royalty of Egypt show them standing very tall, with shoulders back, feet firmly planted on the ground, and long, straight spines. Practice standing tall like an Egyptian queen.

Girl Talk

A girl who's confident has her head up high, and a confident strut! – Mia

Mountain Pose

Mountain pose (below), the basic standing pose in yoga,
is great for thinking about alignment and all your body parts.

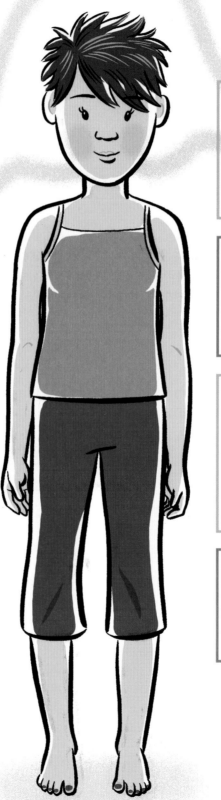

MIND: If you can relax your mind, you can think more clearly and your physical body will respond better.

EYES: Try to keep your gaze soft and relaxed while doing yoga.

SHOULDERS: Sometimes our shoulders tend to round forward or scrunch up by our necks. Try rolling your shoulders back, sliding your shoulder blades down at the back of your body, and dropping your shoulders away from your ears.

LEGS AND FEET: Make sure that your weight is balanced on both feet equally. Your knees should be soft and relaxed. Your feet are separated hip-width apart, and the toes are lined up with each other. Your feet are firmly planted in the ground. You are strong like a mountain.

HEAD and NECK: Balance your head on top of the center line of your body. Dropping your chin forward and down very slightly lengthens the back of your neck.

SPINE: The central support system of your body. Feel your spine get longer as you improve your alignment and stretch yourself taller.

ARMS and HANDS: Keeping your elbows slightly bent and your hands soft and uncurled can help you relax. Relax one body part at a time: fingers, hands, wrists, and up your arms to your shoulders.

HIPS: Balance your hips by not leaning or shifting your weight too far fowards or backwards, or to one side more than the other.

YOUR MIND

Have you ever had a brain freeze? Your mind goes blank because you're really feeling under pressure—during a performance, trying to come up with the right answer in class, or any other time. Have you ever noticed that sometimes it helps to just stop and take a deep breath to clear your mind?

Here's how it works: breathing brings oxygen into your body. Your brain controls the chemicals that cause stress and relaxation. Oxygen and the movement of your lungs help your brain and body respond to stress by sending chemicals that tell them to relax.

✳ **Breathing calms your body.**

✳ **Calming your body relaxes your mind.**

✳ **Relaxing your mind helps you think better.**

Of course we all know how to breathe already! Otherwise we'd be passing out from lack of oxygen. But we don't always breathe in a way that helps our bodies and minds.

Yoga encourages you to pay attention to your breath. Tuning in to something as simple as breathing means you aren't thinking about all the millions of other things going on in your life. Just as your body works better after you've rested it, your mind works better after you give it a chance to relax and take a break, so you can think and concentrate.

Yoga M"ohm"ent

Breathing exercises, called pranayama (pronounced PRAH-NAH-YAH-mah), are an important part of yoga. In Sanskrit, prana means "life-force," and it brings energy to your body. So breathe, increase your prana, and let the energy move through you.

Feeling Your Breath

Sitting quietly in a cross-legged position, lightly rest your hands on your belly (one hand above your belly button, the other hand below).

As you breathe in, fill your belly with air like a balloon. You'll feel your belly pushing against your hands as it expands. Breathe out. As your belly deflates, your hands draw closer in to your body.

Just simply pay attention and notice the movement of your hands on your belly…and wait and watch for the peace and calm to settle on you. Try quietly counting each breath.

Every time your mind wanders, start counting again at one. See how long it takes to get to ten. It's probably harder than you think, but it will keep your mind on the very simple act of breathing.

JUST BREATHE

You breathe about 26,000 times a day! How many times do you actually notice it, though? Being conscious of your breathing is a big part of yoga. Your breath is what gives you life. Picture your breath bringing vitality and energy to your body over a thousand times an hour. Amazing, isn't it?

Mind-Clearing Breath

This breathing technique can clear away the confusion and anxiety you might have just before an important event.

✿ Place your hands on your belly. Now imagine there's a pesky fly on the tip of your nose and you have to blow it off. Stick out your lower lip and with a burst of breath, blow the fly off your nose. Did you feel the quick motion of your belly being pulled back towards your spine?

✿ Try it again, this time with your mouth closed. Inhale through your nose and then exhale forcefully through your nose. Your belly should contract towards your back on each of the exhales. The inhalations happen without really having to think about them, but the exhalations are quick and controlled.

✿ Repeat for ten breaths, and then take a big, deep inhalation and exhalation. If you feel light-headed or dizzy, stop and breathe slowly and calmly. Have you cleared away any of your worries or confusion? Bet you have!

Standing Meditation

Stand tall in Mountain pose (page 13), with your feet hip-width apart. Your shoulders are relaxed and your arms hang loosely by your sides.

Imagine that you are a large sunflower. Your feet are the big sturdy roots of the plant that are deep in the ground. Your spine is the strong stem, and your head holds the pretty petals.

Pay attention to your breathing. As you inhale through your nose, feel the energy of the breath moving in, filling your lungs and moving up your spine.

As you exhale through your nose, feel the breath moving down your body towards your feet. Imagine that your breath is like the water that a flower needs to grow and bloom.

Yoga M"ohm"ent

Gravity is a force that is constantly acting on our bodies—it's what stops us from spinning off into space. Thinking about gravity while standing can actually make you taller. As you feel gravity pulling on you from your feet, your legs feel energized and your spine straightens and lengthens, causing your body to stand a little taller.

YOUR SPIRIT

A lot of yoga has to do with relaxing and letting go of tight areas. Sometimes that can be expanded to opening yourself up to new experiences, and to the world around you. You can open up your heart and mind to new experiences in many ways, such as through volunteering and being more accepting of others. Opening your heart can also mean being generous and more loving: being a better friend, sister, or daughter. Think of the ways that you would like to open up your heart, do better things in the world, or be a more generous friend.

Girl Talk

A true friend is someone who gives back to you what you give to her, in trust and kindness and everything else. – Arden

Open Your Heart

This restful pose opens your hips and heart, and helps to improve the way you feel about yourself.

Sitting tall, place the soles of your feet together, letting your knees fall out to the sides. Place your hands close to your hips on the ground behind you.

Press into the ground with your hands, rolling your shoulders back. Look up. Do you feel a gentle expansion in the chest and throat area? Relax and think about the good things that you have done today.

Yoga Mantras and Affirmations

Mantras are sounds, like ohm (page 7), that are chanted or repeated in a sing-song way. A mantra can help you focus, and can have a huge effect on your mood and energy level.

A popular traditional mantra is ohm shanti (pronounced OHM SHAHN-tee), which means peace. Sitting quietly with your eyes closed, inhale. As you exhale, say this mantra. Repeat three times. How do you feel?

Chanting the traditional mantra sounds can have a powerful effect on your body. But sometimes you might want to use words that have meaning to you. These phrases, or affirmations, can be like a pep talk that reminds you of how wonderful and capable you really are. Try repeating a powerful and positive message to yourself like the one on the right.

Slowly inhale and think: "I am happy."

Slowly exhale and think: "I am healthy."

Slowly inhale and think: "I am lucky."

Slowly exhale and think: "I am loved."

You can come up with your own personal affirmation that you repeat to yourself. Write it down. Be creative. Write or draw whatever inspires you: thoughts, feelings, images, or colors. You can even put it in your yoga journal (page 54).

YOUR YOGA STYLE

Expressing your style can be really important for girls. It can also be confusing. How do we go about getting "style?" Have you ever noticed that girls whose style you admire usually seem at ease with themselves? It doesn't really matter what they look like or what clothes they wear, it's their attitude and confidence that shines through. You can develop your own style with yoga—starting with building strength and confidence in yourself. Although yoga style is not about what you wear, sometimes we need to be practical. Here are a few guidelines for what to wear when doing yoga:

- Choose your favorite pair of relaxed, comfortable pants: simple, stretchy leggings, tights, shorts, or loose and baggy pants.

- A t-shirt or tank top. If your top is loose, be sure to tuck it in for those upside-down moves!

- If you wear your hair in a ponytail, make sure it is tied loosely and low on your neck, since you lie back a lot in yoga. It can be uncomfortable to wear a clip in your hair or have a ponytail right at the back of your head! Ouch!

- A sweater or sweatshirt is good for the end of your yoga session. As you relax, your body will start to cool down.

- It's always a good idea to take your socks off so that you don't slip on your yoga mat or whatever surface you are practicing on. You can put them back on for your final relaxation.

What Color Will You Be Today?
Choosing what you wear to do yoga in can affect your mood. Picking your favorite colors or favorite outfit can make you feel comfortable, energized, happy, or relaxed. Do you have a color that represents your style? What does your color mean to you?

Whenever I am not in a good mood I like to wear my old red sweatshirt. It's really soft and helps comfort me. – Adrienne

Girl Talk

Here are the traditional yoga colors, and the matching chakras and feelings (for more on chakras, see page 11):

Crown Chakra (violet)

This chakra centers on the energy at the top of your head. Think of this area and color when you need to be "on your toes" and use your intuition.

Third Eye Chakra (indigo)

When you have a difficult decision to make, try gently massaging this area in the center of your eyebrows to wake up your senses and instincts.

Throat Chakra (blue)

This is the center of creative energy and expression. When you need to be creative, wear blue around your neck, and express yourself with your voice.

Heart Chakra (green)

Focusing on your heart chakra opens up your feelings. When you need to feel more compassionate towards others, think green.

Solar Plexus Chakra (yellow)

This center for energy and confidence is just above your belly button. For a boost, sit and focus on your breath in your belly.

Sacral Chakra (orange)

This chakra is located at the back of your pelvis. Focusing on this area and the color orange can make you feel more energized.

Root Chakra (red)

This chakra, at the base of your torso, is like the root of a plant that anchors it to the ground. Think about this area and the color red to calm yourself.

IMAGINE THIS...

Relaxing, chilling out doesn't have to happen lying on the couch watching TV. There are other ways to soothe your body, and your mind too. Try tapping into the powers of your imagination. Using your imagination to relax is part of yoga. This is called visualization.

Experience it for yourself. Take a few minutes to just sit or lie quietly. Close your eyes if you want, and let your imagination take you on a yoga journey.

♥ Focus your attention away from distractions.

♥ Focus on your imagination.

♥ Imagine a place where you feel happy, peaceful, and safe.

♥ Let your imagination take you there.

♥ Let those feelings of happiness, peace, and safety calm you and relax you.

Meditation is another way to relax. Any time you sit quietly, breathing softly, resting, and avoiding distractions like the phone, TV, music, and email can be called meditation. What makes this different from just daydreaming (when you zone out and you're not paying attention) is the fact that you are aware that you are doing it. By paying attention to your breathing (feeling every inhale and exhale) and to the feelings that you have, you calm your mind.

Yoga M"ohm"ent

Buddhist monks and yogis can sit and meditate for hours on end. Sitting still, being quiet, and paying attention to their breath for hours (sometimes days) brings great peace and knowledge. Do you think they get in trouble for daydreaming in class?

Girl Talk My favorite place is the beach. Listening to the birds and the waves and feeling the heat of the sun is soooo relaxing for me. – Breeanne

Make Your Own Relaxation Movie

Do you ever feel like there is a movie running in your mind 24 hours a day? It's the movie of your life: all the things you have to do, wish you could do, or already did. It's hard to pause that movie. One way to help is to replace the movie with another, more relaxing one. Here's an example:

✿ **Find a comfortable position. It doesn't matter if you're sitting or lying down—just try to avoid fidgeting or moving. Let your body settle down. Start to notice what is happening with your breathing. Really listen to it and feel it.**

✿ **Pay attention to the sound your breath makes as you inhale and exhale through your nose. Sometimes the sound of your breath can sound like waves on the ocean.**

✿ **Use your imagination to picture yourself lying on the sand on a beach. The sun is warming you. The sand is cradling your body. The waves are making a soothing, steady sound as they softly roll up on the shore. Feel a sense of peace and happiness as the relaxation rolls through your body.**

TWIST FOR ENERGY

Yoga twists are energizing and stimulating. You can do them while lying down, sitting, standing, or even upside-down. Twisting the spine stretches the muscles and releases tension that we sometimes get from slouching or sitting at the computer too long.

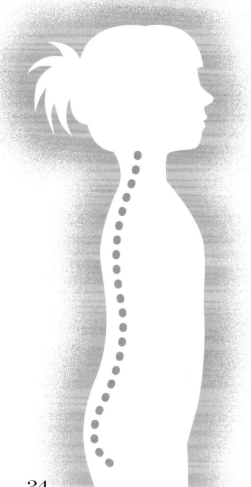

You don't really need an x-ray to see the bones of your spine. Most of us can feel or see them under the skin quite easily. Your spine starts at the base of your neck and travels all the way down to your tailbone. The spine is protected by bones and discs, which is a good thing, because inside the spine are all the important tissues and nerves that help your brain control your body. You can care for your spine by protecting it, and keeping it fit by stretching and twisting.

Yoga M"ohm"ent

In yoga terms, Kundalini (pronouced KUN-da-lee-nee) is the name for the energy that moves up and down your spine. This energy is stimulated to move by twisting and lengthening your spine. It is sometimes described as a coiled snake sitting at the base of your spine. So when you twist, you're like a snake charmer enticing the snake to dance.

24

Seated Spinal Twist

Sitting tall with your legs out in front of you, bring your right foot over your left leg so it sits flat on the floor at the left thigh.

Place your right arm on the ground behind you for support, then hug your right knee with your left arm.

Inhale and sit tall, lengthening your spine from your bottom all the way to the top of your head.

Exhale and turn your head slightly to look over your right shoulder. Stay here for a few breaths. Breathe in and lengthen your spine. Breathe out and deepen the twist…releasing energy all the way up your spine.

Balance out your spine by switching legs (cross the left foot over the right leg) and twisting to look over the left shoulder.

Yoga is definitely different from running around and scoring goals. I like how it's not like dancing, or art, or basketball. It's yoga! – Stacey H.

Girl Talk

FIND THE BALANCE

Trying to balance all the things going on in your life can sometimes have you feeling like you are doing a juggling act on a tightrope. You don't have to be a part of the circus to do yoga, but yoga can help you improve your ability to balance.

Yoga can improve your physical balance—helping you stand strong on only one foot or even on your hands—through building strength, flexibility, and breath awareness. And yoga can also help you with balancing all the day-to-day activities in your life. When things are complicated, hectic, and out of control, 15 minutes of yoga can clear your mind so you can figure out what's really important.

Breathe

Focus

Stand tall

Balance

Yoga M"ohm"ent

Contortionists, tightrope walkers, and other circus performers all have skills that may be developed through yoga. Many performers from the world-famous Cirque du Soleil practice yoga. The increased flexibility and breathing techniques that come with yoga help with their breathtaking feats of balance, strength, and grace.

Tree Pose

Standing in Mountain pose (page 13), focus your eyes on a spot a few feet ahead. Shift your weight to your right leg, raising your left foot off the ground.

Open your left knee out to the side and place your foot above the knee on the inside of your right, or standing, leg. Breathe, focus, and stand tall.

Let your arms float at the side of your body. Then slowly raise your arms up over your head, spreading them out like the branches of a tree.

After a few breaths, float your arms down and return to Mountain pose. Now try it on the other side.

Strike a balance with your poses by always doing on one side what you did on the other.

Variations Just as there are many different kinds of trees in nature, you can have a variety of Tree poses in yoga.

Foot Variation
Keep better balance by leaving your big toe on the floor and placing your foot against your ankle, like a tree with lots of roots.

Arm Variation
Bring your hands together in front of your chest and then straighten your arms above your head, just like the top of a pointy pine tree.

STAND ON YOUR OWN TWO FEET

Are you tired of being treated like a little kid? Do you feel like it's time to start trying things on your own? Doing yoga can be like starting out on the road to independence. Both begin with standing on your own two feet, like in a strong Goddess pose.

As you discover the different postures of yoga, it becomes a game of firsts. The first time you do a backbend, the first time your heels touch the ground in Downward Dog (page 35), or the first time you touch your toes in Standing Forward Bend (page 30). The feeling of gratification that comes with succeeding in a pose is very much like those first few times of independence—when you know you can do something and you feel so proud.

Treat your feet to a massage...with a tennis ball. In Mountain pose (page 13), shift your weight to one foot and place the ball under your other foot. Roll the ball along the arch of your foot and across the toes.

Yoga M"ohm"ent

Your feet are amazing structures consisting of 26 bones and lots of muscles and ligaments. When you are standing, notice your feet. Are they parallel? Are they straight? Are your toes scrunched together? Raise your toes, and slowly lower them one by one, starting at your baby toe. Do they go kerplunk all at once? If you keep practicing this, you'll find that your toes can be exercised and stretched, which feels great!

Goddess Pose

Goddess pose is a strong standing pose.
It can make you feel beautiful, proud, and confident.

Standing tall, spread your legs wider than shoulder-width apart, pointing your toes out.

Bend your knees slightly and lower your hips. Feel the contact with the ground beneath your feet. Your legs feel heavy and strong.

Keeping a tall spine, bend your elbows and raise them to just below shoulder height. Point your fingertips upwards. Your palms face toward your body.

Stay here for a few breaths, keeping your shoulders relaxed and feeling the stretch in your chest and upper back. You are strong and confident and can do anything that you set your mind to.

GO WITH THE FLOW

Water Dance

The following is a series of poses that flow like water. Imagine that your body, breath, and spine are moving like waves as you move from pose to pose.

Start the wave in **Mountain pose** (page 13). Then inhale and reach your arms up overhead, stretching your arms backwards very gently. Imagine you are a giant wave. Exhale and…

…bend forward at the hips to be a waterfall in **Standing Forward Bend**. Bend your knees as much as you want, so that your flat hands can reach the ground. Stay here for a few breaths, imagining your body as a waterfall, with the water flowing down your back. Exhale, then…

…bend and lower to your knees and hands and round your back in **Cat pose**. Breathe out and let your head hang down so your neck is relaxed. Round your back like you are the very top of a wave. Inhale and…

Have you ever felt frustrated because you were trying so hard to do something right and you just couldn't get it? But when you stepped back and relaxed a little, it became so much easier? Like with life, yoga can work best when you stop trying so hard and go with the flow. Just do what inspires you. Dance, move, enjoy.

In flow yoga, a sequence of poses is linked from pose to pose using your breath as a guide. As you enter and exit each position, you inhale or exhale, creating a real connection between movement and breathing. So go ahead and dance to yoga.

Girl Talk

I like how I can seem confident even if I'm not.

Dancing makes me feel good about myself. – Diana

Listening to music while practicing yoga can be distracting or it can help you focus. Everyone is different. Try both ways to see what works for you.

...bend your elbows a little, dipping your belly down towards the ground, and looking up in an arching **Cat pose**. Do the Cat pose movement three times—rounding on an exhale and arching on an inhale—as if you are floating on a group of waves. Exhale and…

…stretch out on your belly to ride the wave in **Bow pose**. Reach behind you to grab the tops of your feet. Press your feet into your hands to raise your thighs, knees, shoulders, and head. Breathe in and out as you rock back and forth like a boat on a wave. Let go of your feet. Exhale, and…

…slide your body back so you're sitting on your heels in **Child's pose**, resting your forehead on your hands. Feel the smoothness of your breath and let your head, neck, shoulders, and back be soothed by imagining soft water rolling down your back.

STRONG BODY

Some yoga poses look like you'd need big strong muscles in order to attempt them. But often smaller, flexible people can hold yoga poses that many strong, muscled people wouldn't be able to do. In yoga, strength comes from breathing deeply and from using gravity to make you sturdy and stable. The more you can relax in a pose, the more you can find the right amount of balance and strength to support you.

Be strong like a warrior. Hold firm to what you stand for. You don't have to be the loudest, tallest, or the most popular person to have strength. Yoga teaches us to have a quiet strength that builds from the inside out.

Warrior Poses

The group of yoga poses called Warrior poses encourage you to build strength by using your breath, gravity, and mind.

Starting in Mountain pose (page 13), exhale and step forward with one leg so your foot is pointing forward and front knee is slightly bent. The back leg is straight and long, with the foot firmly planted, pointing slightly towards the front foot.

Inhale and raise your arms up and overhead, so that your palms are facing each other. Exhale and drop your shoulders away from your ears, creating a long, tall spine.

Feel gravity pulling both feet towards the ground. You have a stable base in the bottom half of your body. Breathe here a few times before you repeat on the other side. You are strong...nothing will knock you over.

Keep trying... *challenge yourself...* *feel proud!*

Yoga poses that build strength are challenging. Challenge can be a good thing when it pushes you to achieve results. But if you get frustrated in a difficult pose, stop, as that is when it can become unsafe and you lose the benefits of relaxation. So if that happens, stop, breathe, gather the strength that you have in you already, and try again.

Girl Talk

When I'm doing a difficult pose, I feel challenged and it makes me want to try harder. – Sharon

Variation

Now change the arm position to try Warrior Two. Lower your arms to shoulder height and turn them so that they are pointing sideways, palms facing down. Turn your head and look at your front fingers. Keeping your back leg strong and stable, feel gravity helping you remain strong. You are a warrior, protecting yourself from harm.

STRONG MIND

It's not just your physical body that needs strength. You use your brain for everything you do. It needs to be strong and healthy so that it works well, too. Yoga can help "exercise" your brain so it works even better!

Inversions (upside-down poses, or any pose where your head is lower than your heart) can help you think better. They change the direction of blood flow, bringing more oxygen (since oxygen is carried around in your blood) to your brain. So going upside-down is like taking a big breath for your brain.

Having a strong mind can also mean that you are confident in what you believe in. We all have beliefs that are valuable to us, and we won't give them up just because other people don't have these same beliefs. Think of some things—like friendship, being truthful, and respecting people who are different—that are important to you. You could even write them in your yoga journal (page 54).

Just as your muscles need exercise in order to stay strong, your mind also needs exercise. Trying new activities and figuring out new things builds smarts. Learning a new pose, or improving one that you already know, can be just the exercise that your mind needs. Challenge yourself, and your mind will get stronger, just like your body!

Downward Dog Pose

This pose creates strength and flexibility in the long muscles of the legs and spine. It also brings energy to your brain, helping your brain work better and helping you think better too!

Begin on your hands and knees, with your hands on the ground directly under your shoulders and your knees directly under your hips. Spread your fingers wide and have nice big paws that are firmly planted on the ground.

Turning your toes under, exhale and straighten your legs, lifting your hips up towards the ceiling. Inhale in this position. As you exhale, gently press into the ground with your hands, and try to get your heels a little closer to the mat.

Don't worry if your heels don't touch the ground. That will come with time. Let your head and neck hang down between your shoulders, keeping your upper body very relaxed. Exhale and lower your knees to the ground.

Arm Variation
You can try this with your forearms on the ground if your wrists feel sore or are injured.

Girl Talk

I tell my friends up front what I stand for, and I don't try something that I know I don't want to do, just because my friends are doing it.
- Sharon

STRETCH & EXPLORE

Once you start doing yoga, you'll be surprised at how quickly you get more flexible. Touching your toes, bending over backwards, twisting...they all come more easily after only a few months of yoga. Most young people are still flexible, but you lose that flexibility as you grow up. Stretching daily is an important part of staying healthy.

As with yoga, you'll never know what you can accomplish in your life unless you stretch yourself to your full potential. Stretching yourself can mean trying new sports or activities, joining a new club, or trying a new art project. Stretching yourself is how you reach your dreams.

Stretch yourself, try new things, grow, and explore!

When you have done a backbend, like Baby Cobra, it is good to balance out that stretch by doing a forward bend soon after. For a nice easy one, try Child's pose (page 39). Standing Forward Bend (page 30) is also a good balancing stretch after a backbend.

Think about something that you've always wanted to try but have never been able to do, for whatever reason. It can be a particular yoga pose, or something wild like flying on a trapeze. You could write it down in your yoga journal (page 54) or even draw a picture of yourself doing it. Think about how you can make that dream a reality.

Baby Cobra

A baby learning how to crawl will do this pose very naturally.
Baby Cobra helps you keep your spine flexible. A flexible spine is a healthy spine,
but it takes lots of time, and it helps to start off slow with this easy beginner backbend.
Take time to stretch your back and spine in Baby Cobra and you'll be amazed how
you will end up exploring all kinds of things you and your body can do!

Lie on your belly, with your forehead resting on the ground and your legs straight out behind you. Place your elbows, forearms, and hands on the floor under your shoulders. Breathe in.

As you slowly breathe out, push into the ground with your forearms, hands, and elbows, continuing to exhale as you slowly raise your head and shoulders off the ground. Don't straighten your arms. Make sure your elbows stay on the ground.

Let your shoulders move away from your ears, as your spine and neck lengthen, and the area around your collarbone stretches. Inhale and lower your head and neck down. Exhale and try it again.

SLOW DOWN

As you grow towards being a teenager, do you ever miss the worry-free, simple life of being a small child? With yoga, those childhood feelings sometimes come back. Doing some of the resting poses can make you feel worry-free, and can make your problems and concerns seem simpler.

Child's pose is a wonderful resting pose. This pose is relaxing and comforting. It gives the sensation of being wrapped up in blankets and tucked into bed, knowing that you are safe and cared for. Resting and breathing in Child's pose soothes the body, quiets the mind, and heals the spirit.

It's really hard to be a girl at this age. It's just stressful!

– Adrianne

Girl Talk

If I'm having a bad day or I'm stressed and go to a full hour of yoga, I feel so much more relaxed and happier. – Stacey H.

Child's Pose

From a kneeling position, lower your hips so you're sitting back on your feet, with the tops of your feet resting flat on the floor. Gently lower your forehead to the ground, and let your arms encircle your head.

Exhale and let the weight of your body rest on your legs. This pose lengthens your back as you sink lower. Feel the stretch in the lower back. Continue to breathe slowly and deeply, stretch and rest.

Your hips might not reach all the way back to your feet. Try tucking a bolster or blanket on your lower legs, under your bottom, and then resting back. Remember, this is a resting pose. Whatever is comfortable is great!

Variations

You can stretch your arms out in front of you.

You can rest your forehead on your arms.

Your hands can lie, palms facing up, beside your feet.

REALLY RELaX...

Relaxing...one body part at a time...is one of the best parts of yoga. Doing a relaxation exercise can help you when you are unable to fall asleep, or when you feel really keyed up and want to unwind.

Sometimes the final relaxation pose in yoga class is called Corpse pose. But don't worry, this pose will actually make you feel alive, refreshed, and rejuvenated. The goal is to lie as still as possible without moving—the way you might teach your dog to play dead. As you get yourself into this relaxation pose, try talking yourself through the following exercise, or have someone read it to you:

Feel the surface below you—the floor, yoga mat, bed, or whatever you are lying on. Picture the building that is supporting it, the foundations. Then imagine the ground below that structure. Picture that structure underneath you, supporting you, keeping you safe. Breathe and relax and let the ground hold you.

Since our bodies cool down when resting, it is nice to prepare yourself for lying back and resting in Relaxation pose by putting on socks or a sweatshirt, or covering yourself with a light blanket.

Girl Talk My favorite place to relax is my room because I can just chill and think to myself. – Joanna

40

Relaxation Pose

This pose can be done by itself but it is also an essential part of every yoga class. Even if you only do one pose, finishing with Relaxation pose is always recommended so that you can feel the effects of the yoga on your body.

Lying on your back, have your legs straight and feet hip-width apart. Your ankles fall open, out to the sides. Your arms lie along the side of your body, palms turned up to the sky. Softly close your eyes.

Feel the contact of your whole body along the ground. Think of how it feels to truly relax and to give in to the idea that something is supporting you. You don't have to do anything. Just let gravity do the work.

Feel your head sinking into the ground. Relax the muscles of your face: around your eyes, nose, and between your eyes on your forehead. Feel the skin of your face relax, your jaw unclench, your lips slightly separate.

Continue to breathe in and out through your nose. Feel the sensation of the air passing through your nostrils and down your throat. Feel your neck and throat relax as your body sinks deeper into the ground.

Variations
If your back is uncomfortable, place a pillow or bolster underneath your knees.

YOGA & SCHOOL

Bringing yoga to school can be as simple as doing some breathing exercises at your desk. No one would even notice, but your body and your mind will!

We all like to do things that we are good at—a fast runner will look forward to gym class and a good reader will look forward to English. Sometimes, though, we dread the things that we aren't good at, for fear of looking bad in front of our friends. Yoga can relax you so that you do your best in everything you try. You can do any of the poses on the opposite page to calm you down before a test or presentation, or to energize you when you feel your attention start to fade.

Yoga M"ohm"ent

By quietly focusing on your breath on a regular basis, it will make it easier when you need to concentrate (like when taking a test). So next time you are stuck on a hard math problem, take a few moments to stop and pay attention to your breath until you feel calm again.

When your eyes feel strained from staring too long at a computer screen or studying or reading for a long time, try this Eye Soother:

Rub your hands very quickly together so that your palms get nice and warm.	Close your eyes. Then cup your hands and place them gently over your eyes.	Hold for a few seconds. Feel the heat from your hands soothe your eyes.	Repeat any time your eyes need a break from the computer, a book, or reading the blackboard.

Here is a simple sequence of yoga poses that you can do at your desk:

Begin with Breathing
Sitting quietly, close your eyes. Relax your eyes, face, and shoulders. Focus on your inhalation and exhalation. Count the breaths in and out.

Chair Twist
Open your eyes. Hook one elbow around to hold the back of your chair (see right). Inhale to sit tall. Exhale and twist, looking over your shoulder. Repeat on the other side.

Cat in a Chair
Sit tall with your feet flat on the floor. Place your hands on your knees. Exhale and round your back, letting your head and neck fall forward slightly. Inhale and look up, arching your back slightly. Repeat the exhale and inhale a few times until your pelvis, back, spine, neck, and head feel loose and relaxed.

Close your eyes briefly, and notice the difference in your breathing, mood, and energy.

43

YOGA & SPORTS

Doing yoga can prepare your body before you skate onto the rink or run onto the field or court. Many pro and amateur athletes do yoga to help their flexibility so they can prevent injuries, to improve their breathing so they don't tire as easily, and especially to work on their concentration so they can focus on doing their best.

Stretching is always recommended as preparation for any sport. Sports-related injuries often happen because we haven't warmed up our muscles properly to make sure that they are more flexible and elastic. Yoga is a great way to permanently improve your flexibility. Better flexibility not only prevents injuries, but also helps you run faster, lunge further, and jump higher.

Yoga also involves the coordination of your breath with movement. As you inhale, you stretch one way, and as you exhale you move another way. In tennis, you exhale as you hit the ball. In soccer, you exhale as you kick. In hockey, you exhale as you shoot the puck. By remembering to exhale on the exertion (the hard part of what you are doing), you can improve your performance in so many sports.

Yoga M"ohm"ent

Striving for your personal best is a part of sports and a part of yoga, too. Sometimes, though, we can get caught up in the competition. One of the main principles of yoga is the idea of doing no harm to yourself or others. You can still strive for a personal best, but without being overly competitive so that others are hurt because of your actions.

Train Your Mind

Warming up the mind before playing a sport can make athletes sharp and in control of their performance. Use breathing techniques, such as Mind-Clearing breath (page 16), that you've discovered in this book to help you pay attention to your breath and re-focus on the task you are performing. This is when you are at your best both physically and mentally—and yoga can help you get into that "zone."

As an athlete, you sometimes feel like you are missing out on things, but sometimes the sport gives you a whole new level of experience and it makes you feel blessed. – Mia

Girl Talk

FAMILY TIME

Now that you're hooked

on yoga, why not introduce it to the rest of your family? Here are some ideas for making yoga a part of your family life.

L-O-N-G Car Trips

Long family car rides can make everyone irritable. Break up the boredom with some seated stretches.

Have everyone (except the driver!) close their eyes and rest their hands on their bellies. They can count ten breaths in and out, feeling the belly pushing into the hand on the inhalation and moving back on each exhalation.

Next everyone can put their hands on their knees. As they breathe out they can round their backs, pressing them into the seat behind. As they inhale, they'll arch their backs and stretch their necks up.

Finally, tell everyone to stretch one arm up over their heads, and the other arm behind their lower backs, bending at their elbows and trying to stretch their fingers towards each other. Switch and repeat on the other side.

Yoga M"ohm"ent

Babies are often yoga naturals. If you have a chance to be around them, watch how they put their toes in their mouths. And have you noticed how even before babies know how to crawl, they practice Baby Cobra pose (page 37) by lying on their bellies and lifting up their head and shoulders? Watching how a baby moves shows us how our bodies used to be before we lost so much flexibility. Just watching them can be inspiring!

Family Squabbles

Arguments between siblings are not too unusual, but why not try some unusual ways to settle the argument? How about enforcing a rule: before someone says another angry word, she must take a deep breath, hold it for a second, and then let out a big, long, slow exhale deep into her belly. Or if you feel yourself getting very angry, try Mind-Clearing breath (page 16). Inhale normally through your nose, filling your belly, and exhale quickly through your nose. At the same time, squeeze your belly back so that all the breath is squeezed out. Do this five times fast, and you just may squeeze out your anger too!

SHARING YOGA with FRIENDS

You can do yoga alone, but some poses, like Boat pose, can be fun when done with a friend. You both get an even better stretch. So grab your best friend, laugh, and have fun, while doing something great for your bodies and minds.

Laughing Yoga

Laughing makes you feel good. It's a fact! When you laugh, you take in more oxygen, which refreshes your brain and body. People who study the effects of laughing have learned that it not only makes you feel better to laugh regularly but it makes you healthier, too! So try some laughing yoga with a friend and see how great you feel.

Ha! Breath

Although the general rule in yoga is to breathe through your nose with your mouth closed, you can practice the Ha! breath with your mouth open.

Sitting in a comfortable position, inhale and fill your belly with air. Exhale and say "Ha!" Do you feel your belly press back towards the back of your body as you exhale? It is a forceful exhalation, as if you are pushing the breath out. The sound that you make is like a silly laugh, and it will make you feel great.

A Yoga Party

Create your own "Yoga Mood Room" with funky pillows and some cool relaxing music, and invite your friends over for a yoga jam. Pop in a few yoga videos (check out ones made just for kids and teens) and share a yoga session with your friends.

Girl Talk A true friend is someone you can always trust, have fun with, and talk to even at the worst of times.
– Breeanne

Yoga M"ohm"ent

Sometimes when you are doing yoga poses you end up gently toppling over, rolling around on the ground, or making funny faces and sounds. Although yoga is often a quiet, relaxing time, it can also be silly and playful. Sometimes people forget how to play as they grow up, and that is too bad, since it's one of the best ways to get exercise and laugh.

Boat Pose

This pose requires cooperation, balance, and concentration. But it can also make you giggle. Have fun!

Sitting facing each other, bend your legs and place the soles of your feet against your partner's. Rock back on your bottom, then reach forward to clasp your friend's hands.

On an exhalation, both of you straighten your legs up into the air, so that your bodies make a V shape. Breathe, and as you exhale, stretch your legs and reach up towards the sky with the top of your head, keeping a nice straight spine and trying to keep your balance.

ENERGY FOOD FOR YOGINIS

Since food equals energy, you need to make sure that you have enough fuel to get you through your busy day. But doing yoga right after a big meal is not a good idea. It can be uncomfortable when you are lying on your front in a pose like Baby Cobra or doing a twist with a belly full of food. First thing in the morning just *before* breakfast is really the best time to do yoga. A few hours after eating your last big meal—after school, before dinner, and before bed—is also good.

Here are some healthy options for a light snack before yoga:

• a glass of fruit or veggie juice

• raisins, a handful of granola, or your very own Yogini Munchie Mix (see recipe at right)

• a piece of your favorite fruit

Yogini Munchie Mix

Have you ever noticed how high-fat snacks like potato chips or fries leave you feeling heavy and drained of energy—or even craving something sweet after? If you want a snack that will give you a great energy boost and that's also good for you, try carrying around your own Yogini Munchie Mix.

Head to the bulk food section with a parent or friend for a yummy variety of healthy, non-perishable snacks. Select four or so of your favorites. Later, mix them and put the mix into little baggies fastened with twist-ties. You can even design your own Yogini Munchie Mix label.

Here are some ideas for what you can put in your yogini mix:

✳ if you don't have a nut allergy, try unsalted peanuts, cashews, walnuts, or almonds (almonds also have calcium, so if you don't drink enough milk, you can eat some extra almonds to help strengthen your bones)

✳ dried fruit: cranberries, apricots, cherries

✳ raisins: try different kinds—golden yellow or big, plump, juicy ones!

✳ granola or a multi-grain cereal

✳ a light sprinkling of mini chocolate or butterscotch chips

Keep some Yogini Munchie Mix with your yoga mat. That way you can always have that little pick-me-up when you really need it!

Fruit Smoothie

Here's a breakfast choice that is light enough for before or after your morning yoga session, but has enough fuel to set you up for that busy day ahead.

✳ 250 mL (1 cup) fresh fruit (your favorite fresh or frozen berries, a banana, or some cut-up apple)

✳ 125 mL (1/2 cup) milk or calcium-enriched soy or rice milk

✳ 250 mL (1 cup) orange juice

✳ 15 mL (1 tbsp.) honey

✳ 125 mL (1/2 cup) plain yogurt (or if using a sweetened yogurt, you can leave out the honey)

Mix together in a blender, and enjoy this easy and healthy breakfast in a glass with a funky straw!

BEAUTY TIPS
FOR YOGINIS

Have you ever noticed that a girl who feels good about herself looks great too? She stands up tall, she smiles, and she walks around with confidence. When you do yoga, you will feel strong and balanced—in tune with your body and radiating good health. When you feel good, you get noticed! People might ask if you got your hair cut or bought a new pair of jeans, but you can just smile and tell them that your beauty secret is yoga.

Breath of Joy

A girl who is happy looks truly beautiful. When you do this exercise, you celebrate the beauty that is in you and around you.

This breath involves inhaling in three stages… and then one big exhale.

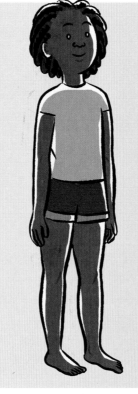

Start in Mountain pose (page 13), standing tall, aligned, and feeling confident and beautiful.

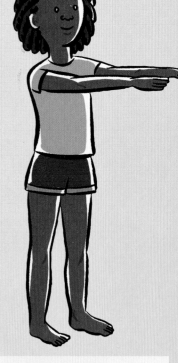

Inhale part way and raise your arms up in front of your chest, palms down.

Pssst! Want to know some beauty secrets from yoginis? These are natural, inexpensive, and chemical-free ways to pamper your beautiful self.

⚬ Add Epsom Salts to your bath. Available from a drug or grocery store, they soothe tired muscles. For a special treat, add a few drops of your favorite relaxing aromatherapy oil, like lavender or sandalwood.

⚬ Witch Hazel is a natural cleanser that soothes and heals the skin. Swipe your nose, chin, and forehead with a cottonball soaked in witch hazel and keep pesky blemishes away.

⚬ Make a Lavender Eye Pillow. You can place this small pillow over your eyes to relax you. Fill a soft, silky sock or knee-high nylon with 500 mL (2 cups) of flax seeds (from the bulk store). Add a few drops of lavender essential oil. Tie up the end of the sock in a tight knot and then decorate with a piece of ribbon or material around the knot. Enjoy the aroma, and let the gentle weight of it soothe your forehead and eyes.

Did you know that stress causes the oil glands in your skin to produce excess facial oils that cause pimples and blackheads? Just one more reason to do some stress-busting yoga moves, breathing, and meditation.

Continue the inhalation and open your arms out to the side as if you are hugging the world.

Complete the inhalation and raise your arms straight up overhead.

Then exhale deeply and loudly, as you fold forward and sweep your arms back down to drop beside you.

Repeat as many times as you want.

CREATE A YOGA JOURNAL

A yoga journal is a great way to keep track of your progress. By writing down when you do yoga, and which poses or breathing exercises you do, you can see how you are progressing over time. But more important, you can write down how you are feeling.

In your journal, draw a picture of yourself in your favorite pose. Label each body part with a positive thought—something that you love about yourself. For instance, your arms might represent the hugs that you love to give, or your shoulders might mean pride in something you have accomplished. Your mouth might be your great laugh.

Making It

Your journal can be any size, shape, or color you like. The pages can be lined to keep your writing neat, or blank so you can write *and* draw. You might want to decorate your journal with bits of material, glitter, photos, colored paper cutouts, art, a personal affirmation (see page 19), or anything else that represents you. You can even keep your journal on your computer.

Yoga M"ohm"ent

Try keeping track of things that make you feel good by writing them in your journal. For instance, when you remind yourself of kind things people have done for you, it might make you feel like doing something nice for others more often. Write down any compliments you have given, or nice things that you have done for other people, too.

Keeping It

Try to write in your journal whenever you do yoga. Describe poses you did, or any breathing or relaxation exercises—even if you just practiced breathing at school or stood in Mountain pose (page 13) while waiting in line for the bus.

Describe your goal for each yoga session. What was your mood before, during, and after? Did any of the poses change how you felt? Did you feel energized, sleepy, relaxed, happy, or sad? Did you daydream or think about a problem that has been bothering you? Writing in your yoga journal is a chance to write down your thoughts, feelings, and moods. It just might make you feel great!

Remember, this is *your* journal, so it can say anything *you* want it to say. Here are some things that other girls have written:

Sun salutations really woke me up this morning. I am so energized. — Sharon

Warrior makes me feel so powerful and strong! — Taylor

My practice felt great today. I'm so happy that I tried something new and stretched in a way that I have never stretched before. — Stacey H.

YOGA & THE WORLD AROUND YOU

After you do yoga for a while, your body starts to feel great and so does your mind. You start to see the world and those around you in a new light too. This is what "awareness" is about. It's thinking about your body, your mind, your relationships, and the world around you in a new way.

From this awareness often comes an urge to make a difference in the world. What does it mean to make a difference? Just being aware of problems and issues that are happening in the world is the beginning of making a difference. But you can also make a difference by giving your time, skills, and energy towards helping to solve problems—whether they are around the world or in your own backyard.

When you do good things for others, not because you want to get something out of it, but because it is the right thing to do, it's called karma yoga. Although it is nice to get praise and thanks when you do something nice for others, a true act of karma yoga is one that is done without expecting anything in return. You can practice karma yoga in your daily life when you show love towards a family member, listen to a friend's problems, help a neighbor, recycle, or volunteer to clean up the local park.

In India, the greeting "Namaste" (pronounced nah-MAH-stay) is used to say hello and goodbye. Sometimes it is used at the end of a yoga class. It means, "I bow to the divine in you." It is a truly beautiful word yogis and yoginis use to show love and respect to others.

Girl Talk

Everyone expresses their beauty when they are truly happy and at peace.

—Stacey J.

Just as doing the poses improves your awareness of your body, and practicing relaxation and breathing improves your awareness of your mind, karma yoga makes you aware of your spirit. You have a special spark that makes you unique in this beautiful union of your body, mind, and spirit.

Namaste.

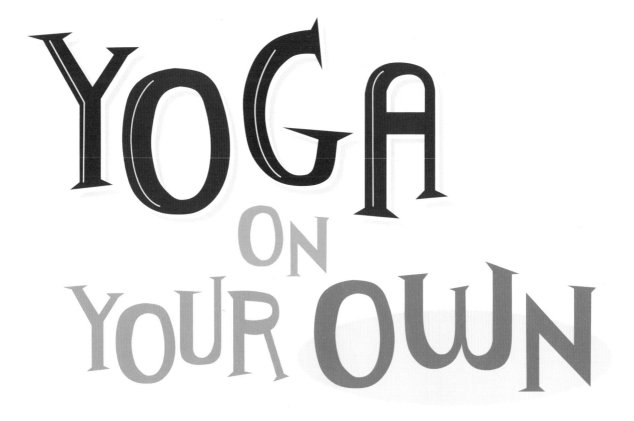

YOGA ON YOUR OWN

Now you've got lots of great ideas for ways to fit yoga into your life. But you might still be wondering how to put these poses together to plan a well-balanced yoga session. The next few pages will give you some more ideas on how to do just that.

As you try out these yoga plans, remember to focus on the motion of your spine and the sensation of movement throughout your whole body. And don't forget to pay attention to how you breathe. If you're not able to notice your breath yet, that's okay too. That comes with practice. Just reminding yourself to breathe and to not hold your breath is a great start.

Take a few minutes before you practice to think about what your mood and energy level are like. Write about it in your yoga journal. It will help you focus on the poses that your body and mind need for that day.

Try to incorporate these elements in your yoga at home:

Breathing Exercises
Spend a few minutes practicing any of the techniques already mentioned in this book.

Warm-up Poses
These gentler stretches prepare your body for the more strenuous poses.

A Balanced Selection of Poses
This includes forward bends, backbends, balance poses, and twists.

Relaxation
Ahhhh....
The best part!

Waking up with the Sun

One of the best ways to start your day is to go to your personal yoga space and just get moving. A sure way to wake up is to do this series of poses called Sun Salutation.

As you inhale, you start in one pose and move to the next on an exhalation. So every movement of your body has a matching breath movement. It is a great way to open up your mind and your senses. So get energized and start your day by greeting the sun.

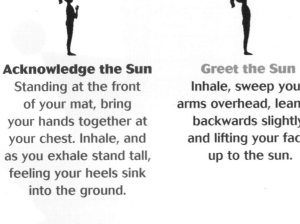

Acknowledge the Sun
Standing at the front of your mat, bring your hands together at your chest. Inhale, and as you exhale stand tall, feeling your heels sink into the ground.

Greet the Sun
Inhale, sweep your arms overhead, leaning backwards slightly and lifting your face up to the sun.

Respect the Sun
Exhale, bend forward at the hips, bringing your hands to the floor beside your feet. It is fine to bend your knees as much as you like so that your hands can reach the ground.

Thank the Sun
Inhale and extend your right leg backwards into a lunge position. Exhale and look up at the sun.

Feel the Ground
Inhale and bring your left foot back, keeping your body in a straight line from your head to your heels. Hold your breath here for a moment.

Thank the Earth
Exhale and bring your knees down to the ground to rest back in Child's pose.

Appreciate the Sun
Inhale and round your back as in Cat pose. Then exhale and lower onto your belly in Baby Cobra pose. Inhale and stretch up towards the sun.

Get Energy from the Sun
Exhale, round your back, and push your hips up in the air, straightening your legs into Downward Dog pose.

Thank the Sun
Inhale and step forward with your right foot, repeating the lunge. Look up and lift your face towards the sun.

Respect the Sun
Exhale and bring your left foot forward to meet the right, coming into Standing Forward Bend with your hands resting on the ground.

Greet the Sun
Inhale and sweep your arms up overhead into a slight backbend.

Acknowledge the Sun
Exhale and bring your arms back down with your hands at your chest, and you're back where you started.

Repeat, but this time step back with the left foot at the first lunge, and then bring the left foot forward in the second lunge. This is one round. Repeat both sides for two or three rounds, or as long as it feels good. You can move as slowly or as quickly as you like, making sure to breathe at each movement. You'll feel warm and energized once you have completed a few rounds.

Anytime Yoga

The following sequence of poses can be done every day, before or after sports, when you wake up, or before you go to sleep. They are safe and simple, and can make you feel alive, healthy, and confident.

Leg Stretches

While lying on your back, bend one leg and place a belt across the ball of the foot. As you exhale, slowly straighten the leg towards the ceiling. Your arms act as a weight on the belt. There should be no tension in your upper body or arms. Let the back of your arms and elbows rest on the ground. Keep your head rested back, and your neck relaxed. Inhale and relax your leg slightly. As you exhale, stretch your leg all the way from your heel to your hip. Flex your foot as if you are standing on the ceiling. Inhale and relax. Exhale and lengthen the leg again. When you are ready, slowly lower down and switch legs.

Cat Pose

Come onto your hands and knees with your hands underneath your shoulders, knees under your hips. Spread your fingers and create nice big cat paws. Keeping your back flat and parallel to the ground, inhale and look up. As you exhale, curl your pelvis under and round your back, dropping your head and

lengthening your spine. Stay here for a few breaths and feel the sensation of the rounded back. On an inhale, release the curve in your spine and curl your tailbone upwards, so that your spine is curving the opposite direction. Relax your arms, slightly raise your head and look upwards. Try it a few times very slowly. Inhale, arch up. Exhale, round your back, relaxing your head and neck and spine.

Child's Pose

Start by kneeling with the tops of your feet flat on the floor, sit back on your heels. Lower your forehead to the ground. You can rest your head on your arms or stretch your arms in front of you for a nice back stretch. Inhale, and as you exhale, sink the weight of your body deeper onto your legs. Enjoy this resting pose.

Downward Dog Pose

Start on hands and knees as in Cat pose. As you exhale, turn your toes under, lift your hips up into the air, and straighten your legs. Keep your hands flat on the floor with your fingers spread wide. Make sure that your feet are about hip-distance apart. Press upwards and backwards with your hips, stretching your spine

and your legs. As you stretch your hips back, lengthen your legs and feel your heels reaching towards the ground. If your wrists start to ache, come down and rest in Cat pose or stretch back into Child's pose.

Lunge

Start on your hands and knees as in Cat pose. Step one foot forward so that your foot is between your hands. Your knee should be directly over your foot. Stretch the other leg out behind you. Your hands can be flat on the floor, on your fingertips, or resting on your front knee. Let the back of your neck lengthen and your spine stretch out. Try not to crunch the back of your neck. Exhale and drop your hips downwards as if gravity is pulling you down. Stay for a few long, slow breaths. Breathing helps your body release and stretch. **Tip:** If your back knee is uncomfortable, put a towel or blanket under it for extra padding. Stop if you feel any pain in the knees.

Relaxation Pose

Complete your yoga session with a few minutes in Relaxation pose.

Relaxing Series

At the end of the day, it's nice to take some time just for you. The following exercises can be done at any time, but are especially nice at the end of the day when you go to your special yoga space. You can think about nothing at all, or think about the wonderful, positive things that happened to you that day. Listen to your breath and feel your body relax.

Little Boat

Lie on your back with your knees to your chest. Wrap your arms around your knees, feeling the contact of your lower back on the floor. Let your hands rest like weights on your legs, allowing your knees to drop slightly closer to your chest. As you inhale, release the weight on your legs and move your knees away slightly. Exhale and draw your knees in towards your chest. Do this with the rhythm of your own breath. Do you feel a sensation of release, of letting go, of relaxing and sinking further into the ground?

Little Boat Twist

Lie back as in Little Boat, hugging your knees in to your chest. Stretch both arms out to the side at shoulder level. Slowly and gently, lower your knees to one side. Breathe, and as you exhale feel a gentle twist in your side and back. Turn your head in the opposite direction to your legs. See if your shoulder can drop towards the ground. If you feel any neck tension, turn your head back to center. Inhale, return your hips and legs to center. Exhale and lower your knees to the other side to twist in the other direction.

Legs up a Wall Pose

Sit with one hip right next to the wall. Start to lean back and as you do, swing your legs up against the wall and swivel around so that your bottom is snug against the wall. Your back is flat on the floor and the backs of your legs are resting against the wall. Rest so that your back is supported along the floor and your legs are supported by the wall. When you exhale, feel your spine lengthen and the exhalation spread right through your legs.

Relaxation Pose

Lie on the floor, with your knees bent, arms at your sides, palms up. You can place a bolster or cushion under your knees and let your legs rest on top. Breathe in and out through your nose. Close your eyes. Relax your face and the back of your body. Let your inhalation happen naturally, and your breath move through your body naturally. Relax and just be aware of your breath.

MORE ON GIRLS' YOGA

Doing yoga in your own oasis can be special. But you may find that you would like to try it in a class setting, too. A yoga instructor can make sure that you are doing the poses safely and correctly. She can also help you to challenge yourself and try new things. By going to a yoga class you will also meet other girls like you who want to stretch their bodies, open their minds, and have fun!

Here are some ideas to help you find a yoga class that's right for you:

Ask your teacher if you can do yoga in gym class, or your school might have an after-school yoga program.

Try your local recreation center or YMCA. There may be a variety of types of yoga classes you can take.

Most cities have yoga studies and classes devoted to kids or teens. Try the website www.yogafinder.com to help you find yoga studios in your area.

There are lots of different types of yoga. Think about what you are looking for, and check out the type of class that is right for you.

Hatha Yoga – Hatha is the general term for the type of yoga that uses yoga poses. When a class is advertised as simply "Yoga" or "Hatha Yoga" it usually refers to a general kind of yoga class that focuses on a variety of yoga poses as well as some breathing and relaxation.

Ashtanga Yoga – This is sometimes called "Power Yoga." It is a very physical type of yoga. It is great for building strength and challenging yourself. Just make sure to choose a class at a beginner level and go at your own pace.

Flow or Vinyasa Yoga – This type of class focuses on linking the poses together using your breath, so that you flow from pose to pose. Nice if you like to move, dance, and feel energized.

Iyengar Yoga – This style of yoga focuses on the proper alignment of your body when doing the yoga poses. It's great for people who want to work on strength as it is challenging and uses props to help with the poses.

Bikram Yoga – This is yoga that is done in a very hot room since heat loosens up the muscles and helps them stretch more. This is a challenging type of yoga...maybe one to try out after you have practiced yoga for a few years.

Recommended Books & Websites

For more on yoga poses:

The Complete Idiot's Guide to Yoga
**By Joan Budilovsky and Eve Adamson
Alpha Books (2003)**

Yoga for Children
**Mary Stewart and Kathy Phillips
Simon and Schuster (1992)**

Yoga and You
**Esther Myers
Shambhala / Random House (1997)**

www.yogajournal.com
This website has articles on yoga, and lets you search for poses

For more on meditation:

*Just Say Om!:
Your Life's Journey*
**By Soren Gordhamer
Adams Media (2001)**

Special thanks

to all the girls who contributed to this book:

Arden Azim
Natalie Baylis
Mizzú Bodó
Alex Castator
Taylor Castator
Michelle F.
Sharon Fichman
Laurie Fletcher
Adrianne Ghebril
Mia Gordon
Adrienne Hall
Kimberly Hamilton
Stacey Herberman
Stacey Johnston
Hannah MacArthur
Joanna Minakakis
Nikki Petsis
Tereka Tyler-Davis
Rachel Wallace
Diana Wright
Seacy Zhen

Thanks to the fellow yoga teachers who reviewed it:

Paola di Paolo
Monica Voss
Denny Wise

And thanks especially to editor Anne Shone, whose dream and commitment both to yoga and this book made it possible.

Index